MW01715427

The Light Beyond The Stars

Valerie Savage

To Liza

Valerie A. Savage

Journey of a Dream Press

The Light Beyond the Stars

© Valerie Savage 2017

All rights reserved. No part of this book may be used or reproduced in any manner whatsoever without written permission from the author, except by a reviewer who may quote brief passages in a review.

Written by Valerie Savage

ISBN: 978-0-9897142-5-9

This is a work of fiction. Any resemblance to any person living or dead is purely coincidental.

This book was printed in the United States of America

Journey of a Dream Press

PO Box 1565

Duluth GA 30096

www.journeyofadream.

Dedicated to
Eugene C. Savage
and
Delores A. Savage

Perhaps it is my obsession with the night sky. My thoughts project out for a closer look at the reality I know is there in the stars. Something is causing me to be here in these stars. It is here, beyond time where I no longer feel I am squandering the minutes; here is space where I can truly feel my existence. Where can this place be? I know no words to describe my existence now. I long to be in no other place than where I am now.

I started from the stars but have gone to a distant dimension beyond any boundaries I have ever felt, I call it oblivion, infinity, the eternal now. This is the now and it is oblivion. I am here now. What were the last actions I took before I came here? I cannot remember. I feel myself float to the Eternal Now. This is oblivion, yet the degree of freedom feels as if there are still boundaries. If it truly is the Eternal Now, there would be no boundaries. It would be transparent off to infinity. But I do feel a boundary, a longing for something other than here. Yet I only have the here within the eternal now.

Oh! Look at the stars in the night. From here I can see so many other places. The pinpoint of my existence is here, yet the pinpoints of many other existences are many other places, scattered through the universe. Jesus said, "In my Father's house are many rooms." I am only now discovering how large this house is. In this eternal now is a degree of freedom, for my thoughts are freer than they have been for a very long time. I try to tap the edges of this freedom and it scares me as to how far I can go. What was my last action? I cannot remember what it was. Not long ago on the path of time I was trying to escape from something.

Oh! The stars are moving before me in the night. Look! This is my star for it opens up to me. I feel it and I open back to the star. Tears begin to flow from my eyes. My precious night, my precious star, my ascent from oblivion is beginning. I feel the breakage of time fold its borders around me, bringing me back to limited time and bordered space.

My last action stabs into my mind. The memories come flooding back, filling my senses with pain. My thoughts try to pull me back for an escape to the place of oblivion.

"I'm leaving you for someone else," I told my husband. He was angry, so angry. His petty control lost as a room in the Father's house vacated. One of our children is married and working on her career. The other child is in college. It was the first time we had to face each other as grown up adults. The disappointment was great for both of us.

We had our protective routine to maintain our reality. We existed in the mundane, and it shielded us, protected us from any greater truths. I was the one that wanted to find meaning in those greater truths. I began to explore as I pushed on our boundaries. My sense of self expanded out to greater possibilities and greater realities. I found courage to explore my greater service in the universe and to dare express that service. He was so angry.

The stars open up for me, opening my heart wider and wider. I can feel the love in the night. My husband insisted on knowing the identity of this person who dared to enter our reality and break our safe routine. He was not prepared for the safety coating to shatter; this was his safe world. If his safe world shattered, his emotional bonding from the inside out would shatter too. Yet I spoke the name, the sacred name that came from deep within me. From a love that I knew could still be there, I whispered, "Luke."

I remember now. That was my last action. That is why I am lying on the deck looking up at the stars. I feel coldness enter my body suddenly as a new reality sets into my thoughts. I roll over and see blood on the floor. There was no pain when I was in oblivion, but I am no longer in oblivion, and the pain sears throughout my body as I scream.

But then the stars come back, shining so brightly into my heart. The oblivion is a beautiful eternal now as the distant sound of an ambulance comes from another room in my Father's mansion.

Time passes as I lie on the deck. I see one star shining brighter than the other stars and I am compelled to be nearer to this star. I feel my thoughts rise up to that luminous point. I feel its burning light around me. The pain is gone! The deck is far below me, where I lie in a pool of blood. Yet I am above the deck, looking down. I am scared, but soon that feeling is soon replaced by acceptance, and the fear disappears. The throbbing pain is gone. Thoughts of my husband are only a distant memory. I do not hate him nor do I love him; he was only there playing a part.

Then I think of Luke. My heart melts and suddenly I am with him as he climbs into his bed. I lie next to him. "Luke my love," I whisper in his ear. He does not turn to hug me but instead he cries. "Why are you crying?" I hold him close but he turns away. I tell him that my husband knows about us now

"I will leave him," I whisper, "And then you and I can live together." But Luke continues to cry. The news must simply be too overwhelming for him. I relax and fall asleep next to him.

I awake to peace in my heart. There is a light that shines bright but does not blind my eyes. I stand up, but there is no feeling of weight. I know Luke is not here, I am some place other than at Luke's. My body rises and floats to the heavens. I suddenly stop floating. I sense a being next to me, I am not sure, I feel so confused. I look over but still cannot see her face. I just know it is female. What brought me here? It does not matter, and I don't care. I just want to drink in this peaceful feeling, this deep awareness that everything is well within itself. I cannot think of a thought or emotion that could be other than what now exists in this peace.

I raise my hands and find that they are translucent. I am light shining. How beautiful they appear; evidence of age is gone. I see swirls of energy. This is what is stopping me from seeing the face next to me. It is the translucent swirling light. I use my shining hands to touch her arm and a rush of intense energy shoots up my hand and through my body.

"Who are you," I ask, "or what are you?"

"I am here for you as you transition."

"And where am I to transition to, and from what?"

"Back to your energy body, back to a truer you, for you have left your physical body behind as you no longer live the life of Jessica Ann Johnson."

I know this must not be for I remember sleeping next to Luke. Now I am here in this … where is this place? What is happening to me? Fear rushes through me causing me to be very cold.

"Come with me, my child." she whispers softly.

Her tone is reassuring, like a mother giving directions. In my confusion, I follow her into a room with a large empty platform.

"Please sit here."

I turn to look, and I find two chairs. I sit down in total bewilderment. Above me, stand my parents. They look so young. My father holds me in his arms. I am a baby. I turn to the entity next to me. "What is this about?"

"Just watch. You will understand soon."

My thoughts go racing. I am in a dream. That has to be what is happening. This cannot be solid reality, so it must be a dream. If this is 'real', then this is beyond my comprehension to take in and process. My memories, though, keep telling me what was real to me. A powerful gentle force draws me back to watch the stage.

"As you watch yourself," she says beside me, "you will understand your experiences in greater depth than you could when you were only the participant." She is right. I could have made different choices as Jessica Ann.

I see the pain and suffering I felt when I was a teenager and my first friend, Lana, left me—or, to be more honest, when I left her. I was, as teenagers frequently are, self-absorbed and self-righteous. My friend and I knew how the world should be. We were going to help people in medical need. I planned to be a physical therapist and Lana wanted to go into obstetrics. We were coming back from a party where we'd each had one glass of wine. It was late when she dropped me off, but I wasn't worried. She only had three miles to drive home. It was a deer, a part of nature. It jumped out in front of her car. She swerved, and her car went over an embankment and rolled four times. They said it was her lack of experience. I said it was unfortunately fate. Hours later, Lana's mother called my house and then the police.

She was alive when they found her, but severely injured. The permanent change in her made a permanent change in me. Her brain injury made her almost like a baby. I stopped in several times to visit her at her parents' house. Her mother and I made a day of it as I helped wash, dress, and put makeup on Lana, but then I gradually began to drift away, to show up less and less often. I do miss my old friend, but I see that I could have made a different choice—not to drink at the party, perhaps—that would have saved her from her present quality of life. She could have made a different choice, too. She did not, and I did not. We choose the situations we make and we create from those choices.

The scene before me shifts. "Daddy," I breathe as I watch my father give me a Popsicle on a hot blistery day. He is so young, so vibrant. Why did I never see that before?

My mother, just as young and luminous as my father, holds me tight as I cry that day I fell and skinned my knee. "Oh, Mama, how could I not have known how wonderful you were?"

I watch myself take a job that was secure and financially sound, but dull and uncreative, or so I thought at the time. I had searched only for security and had pushed aside my intuitive nature, which would have guided me through life. There is a time to be on earth with your feet on a path of certain outcome, and then there is a time to escape into the ethers of possibilities and lighten the load. My job back then entailed customer service for an insurance company. I dealt with people who'd had their lives disrupted and were under great stress. I'd take a problem and try to solve it with the best resources I had available. I learned to talk to insureds, claimants, legal staff, and appraisal people. It became a time I was learning many things. But there came a time when I was not learning nor was I growing. So, I ended it.

I feel my accomplishments and the joy I've caused. But I also feel the pain. The pain I caused my husband when I shut him out of my life, despite the deep love he and I had felt when we were first married.

I feel my love for Luke. I see the love of parents, partners, family, friends, and I see that every bit of love I chose to share carried conditions. The love was always there, but I put conditions on it, terms, limits. I had access all along to unconditional love, love without limits. Now that I was here in this dream, I could see that great flow of love pouring through all beings, continually creating life, power, existence. Why did I never tap into that divine river?

I stand abruptly.

"Who are you," I plead, "and what am I doing here?"

"My name is Shanderia. As I told you, I am here to assist you in transition."

"What transition? From what to what?" But even as I ask it, I know that this is only a dream. I need to remember it, though, for it is greater than any dream I've ever had.

"You are moving from your life as Jessica Ann Johnson," Shanderia says, "into your energy self. You chose to experience life as Jessica Ann, so you could learn lessons and experience joy. That life ended, rather abruptly, which is why you are still not accepting this transition easily.

"I died? Are you telling me I'm dead?"

Shanderia smiles. "You simply changed rooms."

Her voice is so calm, so reassuring that I think perhaps I am not merely dreaming. She's read my mind. That's where she got this analogy about my Father's house.

She smiles again and nods. I've always wondered about telepathy, the direct transference of thoughts, images, and feelings; it is so much less cumbersome than speaking. But Shanderia seems to understand that I still need words. They feel more comfortable to me. I see her lips move as she talks to me in my mind. "This is your transition."

Sadness fills me. I won't ever be Jessica Ann Johnson again. "You're saying I've gone to another room?"

"You are Jessica," Shanderia says, "but you are also many other beings. It is all you, the real you. This you has many more degrees of freedom than your physical self."

"How can this be so?" I ask because I want more proof. I'm not quite ready to understand this experience my soul seems to be having.

"Close your eyes, my dear, and think of something you desire to see before you."

I close my eyes and see myself embracing Luke. Like a movie, I see the whole life I would have had with him. I see how love-tainted my sight was before. I ignored his obsession with work, with golf, his self-absorption. I ignored the way I felt left out of his life, because at the time, it didn't matter since I was married to another man. It fit well into my life situation at the time. But now I see what our life together would have been like. I see us going through life working on some issues but letting others slide by as we grow old together. Luke passes away first. Our adopted child, now an adult, assists me in moving out of our house of twenty years. She is a good child and we have a deep bond that helps me in the loss of Luke. She is my best friend.

I open my eyes. Was I hypnotized? I breathe hard, trying to catch my breath, grasping for something familiar. My thoughts are swirling.

"I could have had a full life with Luke." My heart is pounding. "I saw it, I felt it!" I still feel the memories. A bubble of reality I could have followed but did not. No, I woke up; I am here now without my daughter. I suddenly remember Shanderia and the purpose to this experience.

I step back from this dream as I get up out of the chair. I realize even if we get our deep desires that those desires, will in one way or another end. I look at Shanderia, drinking in her wisdom.

"Everything ends, doesn't it? Everything ends." I stare into the distance.

"I could have had a full life with Luke.

"You could have had a full life with your husband as well," she says, "if you had made different choices." She smiles warmly. "Everything that has no eternal substance to its form will end. You can experience lessons of life in your mind, feeling the emotions as well as sensing the scene and thinking the thoughts. You can manifest immediately any desire you wish. But if your mind is not in alignment with your soul, those manifestations will be from your created ego. Anything from ego will always be limited and create consequences that will manifest immediately or later."

"Consequences?"

"Yes. Humans tend to label them as either good or bad, as heavenly or evil, but really, people ultimately find whatever it is that comes from their hearts. You may try to find the God reality or you may judge harshly. Either way, this is ego, ideas that are still of limited concepts."

I try to imagine what she means. I judged my husband harshly. I judged a lot of people harshly. "Are you saying I should have looked for good in everything around me?"

"There was good in everything, whether you chose to see it or not."

"I don't understand. What do you mean?"

"This idea of separation—the thought that says parts of us are evil and parts of us are heavenly—is still three dimensional, limited. These ideas can create heaven on earth or can justify atrocities, and all the time, the people thinking those thoughts have a deep belief in the good intentions of their own hearts. The 'I' and the you, the good and the bad, the us and the them; these are all broken symmetry."

I think back to the times I read about knights fighting, killing and maiming, all in the name of saving souls. How base human thoughts enter into many ideologies of faith. It cannot be the highest and best good by those being killed for their own belief, their own outlook on life. Those who have the best of intentions in their hearts will fare better than those with tainted lying hearts. Can a person truly believe they are saving another soul by killing them? Maybe this is better than killing someone because of greed, sex, revenge, or power, but it eventually comes down to judgment by God within one's soul. Only within will the truth be known.

Can it be that as one develops awareness, one can see the truth deeper and deeper in another's soul, in their energy field?

"You're right." She's reading my thoughts again. "That is a good example of the broken symmetry that is trying to bind itself together again. You are developing an awareness to know, to be, and to shift back to your true Self. As you experienced, even your deep desire has an end from your created thoughts. Yet here you are, free from limited feelings of lack."

I sit back in the chair and watch the rest of my life as Jessica Ann Johnson unfold before me. I can see the great lesson transpiring from this life expression. I missed seeing the highest and best in others and many times sold myself short of my full potential in life. My original intention, I see now, was to express myself. I see I picked my parents and all the other characters in my life in order to see a greater truth. I shudder, though, as I watch myself being Jessica Ann Johnson. I practically vibrate as my life story ends before me and I am where I have started this dream. I see my soul-self leave her physical body; I see my dying self-pass into streaming light, to the here and now.

"Shanderia, if I'm dead, how can I still be here as me?"

"You are you, but a much more unlimited you now that you've left Jessica Ann's body behind."

"May I go back and do it differently?"

"You may," she says. "But why go back into that stream of reality, when you can go on to another level of vibration to understand the different aspects of your past life's deeper meaning? We are not linear beings and as such can travel the time of perceived linear experiences, into the past or into the future. We create however we wish to create whenever we wish to create. We can live lives that are in different points of time, different aspects of space." She spreads her arms wide, as if to encompass the universe. "It is all happening simultaneously," she says. "Now."

"How did you get to be so wise?"

"Wisdom?" Shanderia's voice is gentle. "We are all wise, but some of us do not know it yet. We create the ego when we individualize vibration from the whole into an individual expression, thereby creating a broken symmetry. A drop of water is only a small part of the ocean, but it holds the entire ocean within itself. Just so, it is inside us to be able to comprehend our being. Even though a drop of water would have a difficult time comprehending the vast ocean, all the properties of the ocean are in that drop. The ocean is made up of individual drops of water. The drop in its separation cannot understand the vast unity of all the drops that create an ocean."

"I'm just one drop? Is that what you're saying?"

"As Jessica Ann, you were an individual spark of energy. That individualized vibration began to learn about a perception of separation. You perceived loneliness, a sense of yourself as being lesser or greater than others you came in contact with, and you experienced fear for your survival. All these feelings came from separation from the whole."

I looked around me. "But I wasn't really separated, was I? I only thought I was."

"You're certainly right about that," Shanderia said. "And that sense of separation leads to the creation of greed, lust, anger, revenge. It justifies every single one of those elements. In fact, it justifies anything it perceives as necessary for its 'I'. An individual's first desire creates the first break from symmetry. After that," she paused and smiled widely, "it's all downhill. The primal desire may be to go back to the whole in the Highest Spiritual Energy, but humans seem to have an unerring ability to thwart that desire."

"The way I did," I say, and she doesn't refute me.

"Each individual energy travels many paths that lead to many finite existences. There is a great calling in the depths of each small drop. The structural vibration deep within itself keeps yearning for something more. The thirst of the individualization is great as the dream enters into its being, whispering that there is something greater, and if you seek it, you will find it. It creates desire that creates activity in the physical realm."

I think back to the movie-like quality of Jessica Ann's life. "It sounds like you're saying such activity doesn't accomplish anything."

"It accomplishes a great deal, but it is all finite activity; a created beginning and a created end. There is a deep desire to continue in finite activity. Yet each water drop—to continue our analogy—truly seeks the soul, with its infinite love, infinite compassion, joy and harmony. The soul is pure light expressing. When this pure Light expresses, self is no longer merely self, but ultimately is its true perception of union with the whole. The vibration rests secure in pure Light, and the need for created elements disappears, since such elements are false. There is no lack, no need, and no desperation from self. Desire actually comes from the Light."

"But I thought you were saying that desire was bad?"

"Desire is like a prism. It disperses the light and shows its infinite variety. When it comes forth, it creates the physical reality. The prism, the filter, is a guide to the Light as it manifests. The individual simply expresses this reality as it filters through."

"I was nothing but a filter?" I thought back to my life as Jessica Ann. "I must have accumulated a lot of sludge."

She laughed. "What you are doing now is cleaning your filter. The cleaner the filter, the brighter the manifestation of the pure Light of God. Light from God creates life in its pure form at every eternal moment. We can, and on a certain level we do, perceive Light in its purest form to be the One. Our perception of One in Light leads us to an ever finer vibrational purity."

While I'm trying to make sense of all this, Shanderia hands me a book. I study her face for a moment and then open the thick volume.

It's all there. Jessica Ann Johnson and her youth, my/her struggles in high school, her search in college, finding work, trying out various relationships. I thumb through the book and sense it all coming together into a time of peace and acceptance of what has been unfolding before me. How did this book come into my hands? It is more than just words. As I look through it, I experience all the information deep within my being.

Shanderia moves closer to my right side. "Do you see now, my dear?"

"I do." I feel the bliss of life flowing through me, but something tells me this is not all I am to learn. "You're going to show me more aren't you?"

We both know there is so much more.

I close the book. There are many more books, before and after this one. "These are lists of all my experiences, aren't they?"

"Yes," she says with a slight shrug. "They are your consciousness experiences."

"When do the finite experiences end?"

"Whenever you wish them to end. You create as you observe and in your creating you find wisdom. You create and the Source of all Creation responds. You've created the library to comprehend the vibrational energy of experiences you can draw upon. It is easier for you to understand a book with a beginning and an end, instead of trying to see vibrational energy existing as manifested information. "

I walk along the library, running my fingers along the rows and rows of books. The shelves seem to be unending. Contemplating all these conscious lives, I begin to hear Shanderia tell me these are not only my lives but other lives as well, splintering into experiences upon experiences. She says on higher levels there is no separation of selves.

I slowly return to the book that is Jessica's life. A feeling of comprehension and joy fills me as I reach out and touch this book. The energy I call love comes flowing through me at this moment. Waves of pure Light roll through my being. Once again I am sitting in the chair.

Shanderia's voice comes floating over. "You are now experiencing the completion of your mission. It is now time to experience the finer vibratory self that you were before you experienced Jessica."

"I remember," I say. "I saw her in my dreams, but I thought she was an angel."

"It was you, but you simply didn't understand."

"I felt her advise me when I was really sad."

"Of course. She was the finer vibratory part of yourself. She was you."

It feels like weight melting away, an intensity of light and awareness opens up all the cells of my existing body. I can see the breath flowing in and out of this new lighter body. There are intense lights of different colors swirling around me. There's a sound, too, but unlike any I've ever heard before. It plays in harmony with the flow of the light. There are bands of light, folds of light, light appearing as angel's wings, auras of light that interweave lattices in connecting lines, light going in and out of my perception. I know the resounding tones are pure Love. Love beyond any understanding I had in my physical experiences; it is an incredible all-encompassing love. I bathe in this total experience.

I see the opening I came through. It is lime green, alive in active hues, tinting the space as my awareness flows through. It is my self, yet there is no self. I am in the flow of light energy for I too am a purity of light flowing with the hues. "This is heaven," I think. "This is heaven!"

Shanderia now appears in my realm of thoughts in glowing hues of blue, gold, white and violet, just the way I first saw her. I was unable to make out any detail hidden among the swirls of energy, but I know it is her.

"Welcome to your return my dear."

"Is this heaven?"

"It is what many people on earth would describe as their perception of heaven. But the concept is too limiting for this state of energy. It is your truer self, a finer vibration, an existence that has always been you, but not you. It is a place you and many others have known in your hearts. A place you dream of in the spring sun, a place in the stars as you seek refuge. It is not a point of reality in the four dimensional realms. It is a place beyond boundaries of such things as space or time."

"But it feels so real."

"People seek it and desire to express it in art, music, literature, or mathematics. Some use philosophy or religion, trying to capture the moving energy into a solidification of Spirit. It is like cutting a flower. It may be beautiful for a short time, but it will begin to wither and die as soon as it is cut off from the creating Source." She waves her hand as if to encompass all I've just seen. "This is your Self. You had only a glimpse of it when you were Jessica Ann Johnson, for you were solidified in a brief moment of eternal time. Now, though, you can move beyond the dream of the dreamer or the vision of the artist. Although you perceive this reality as limitless heaven, it has boundaries and laws. The boundaries are much broader, though, and the laws more refined in responsibility. The creation has much more freedom in its manifestations."

The flow of energy that is around me reaches far and I know I am expanding out to new, seemingly boundless realities. The flow of energy intertwines with one line of light as it begins and another ends. I feel a perception of 'I', but it is just a faint shadow in the lines of light, and I am unaware where they begin or end in this dance of vibration. The essence that is Shanderia comes before me and I know her intention, to guide me and teach me, to assist in my growth back to the whole.

She leads me to a place where energy flows in a circle. I enter this circle and again I feel this overwhelming existence of love, acceptance, and incredible power. Light speaks to us and directs us. I can distinguish other energy forms as well, dancing in this circle. There is a transparent wall around us, but it is alive with energy, energy that is reflecting our dance. I flow effortlessly into this swirling dance of light.

Beyond the wall I see Shanderia's smiling face. Her thoughts reassure me. "The circle is a renewal process. Your spirit traveled far in the previous lifetime, and you dance now to integrate all the energies of your soul's experiences with the whole."

I understand. I feel that everything is balancing. I am light energy dancing with other light forms, flowing through the circle. I think of myself in the form of 'I' and more energy begins to take forms as separate beings. The dance continues and I know Shanderia is near. As I take more form and those around me take more form, the dance becomes less flowing and more cumbersome. All the images are so beautiful with their waves reflecting through their body forms. The joyous dance continues. But the reflection of the light dims as each body takes on more details. I begin to sense the feelings and thoughts of the other beings. We are becoming more like individuals, but we still radiate the light as it filters all around, weaving in and out, and filling all the spaces.

A harmonizing sound from within our circle grows and seems to melt within me so that I expand out, spiraling to a point high above our beginning point. As we melt together into a powerful force, I sense love in its purest form. There is no perception of 'I' yet we are expressing in individual forms. The love grows from All that Is, and merges us into One. The individual 'I' fades and we are One in Love. Our energy vibrates with love that is truly endless–there is no sense of boundaries. It is only flowing energy of crystal pure love.

"This is how universes are created," Shanderia's voice sounds from all around me. "Love is the basis of creating all physical forms and physical energies. It is the basis of creating other dimensions with greater degrees of freedom or lesser degrees of freedom. It is thought reality. Thought is almost instantaneous manifestation, moved by emotion. We express as beings of thought, and we change with our thoughts. We are expressions of dynamic feelings."

"How is this possible," I ask, even though I know in that moment that possibility is a constant in this feeling of Love.

"A form can feel an emotion," Shanderia says. "You create a scenario from that perceived emotion. Can you sense the excitement on the physical form as the energy emerges?"

"Yes. Oh, yes."

"Your perceived creations are bursting forth into manifested actions. The responsibility of creation is great as the freedom is great." Shanderia's voice seems to vibrate within me.

I understand now why one must reach this place with cleansed thought forms. I return to a perception of my body, seeing my hands, my feet, my legs. I see the others as well, still engulfed in swirls of light coming into visual form.

"My child…" I hear Shanderia's voice in my head.

"Yes, I am here." I can barely speak. I walk back with her, and she holds my arm to stabilize me. Or am I really walking? Doubt enters my mind.

There before me is a beautiful building. It is round with no doors. Gardens with sparkling plants vibrate with incredible colors. As we approach the building translucent colors swirl from the outer shell and a deeper color lurks behind. Beautiful violet light forms a door, and we enter a room so large that I have the feeling of being just a speck on the floor. Opening beyond this room is a hall lined with columns. I see light coming from the room ahead. The vibrant light shines on plants and reflects from the sparkling beauty of a waterfall. Never have I seen such brilliance and depth. "I remember such things from my life on earth," I say, "but they never appeared in such glory!"

"The glory was there all along," Shanderià says, "but your humanized filter refused to see it."

The light pulses as my thoughts of earth dim again.

"Blessed child – please come this way," and she leads me behind the towering plants and past the waterfall.

There sitting in a circle are people I knew from my life as Jessica Ann Johnson. My husband looks at me and I at him. There are no feelings of anger, hate, or even revenge between us. There is simply a nod of understanding. He smiles and says, "Perhaps I went too far, but I'll work this out."

I feel compassion for him as he speaks, and I send him love. He sends love back to me.

I see the daughter I never had, the one I experienced in the vision of my life with Luke. "Oh Aggie," I breathe, feeling the deep pure love as she gazes at me. There is Melinda, my sister and Bill, my brother smiling. "Well done," they say, and I know that each of us deserves those accolades. There are my lovely children–Jack, Andrea, and Johnny–sending me love and accepting the love I return to them.

Oh! Luke I see the light and love flowing in rushing exchange, not as in the earth life but as a stronger encompassing love. Yes the love on earth is an expression of the love that is here in this place of greater love. This love transcends power issues; there is no sense of great desire, only a wish to express love in pure form.

There are so many beings in this circle. I see the light tie each of us together. An ethereal tone harmonizes our thoughts and emotions, and we appear in a group of love. I know we have been together for a very long time, for many lifetimes.

“Thank you, Shanderia,” I whisper, and join in the thoughts of the group as we consider the past life and what we have learned from it.

I see my life as Jessica Ann woven through with themes, such as a yearning to find pure love in physical form. I tried to express loyalty from the heart, and I learned the importance of being true to my inner nature and of forsaking the dictates of outer influences as a deciding factor. All the people in the group reviewed these memories with me. Purity of love was the theme that rang the loudest. It first appeared as I was a baby coming out into the world. I see that at that moment of birth, I was not far from the place I’d left. I saw myself as a child exploring the world around me with an open heart and interacting with my parents. As I grew, the idealism of my youth tried to find a pure love out in the world. As an adult I sought that great love in another person, with Luke.

My brother speaks, breaking into my thoughts, but somehow not intruding on them. “Do you see that you were at first a vibrant expression of love in purity? But as you lived your life you turned that love outward. In trying to replenish that love that you thought you had lost, you began to look outside yourself. Where was that pure love?”

A strong image comes into my thoughts; a fear that Jessica Ann would not find that pure love again. “I almost stopped believing in it,” I say.

“But you do not possess the love,” Bill says. “You are the love. The love is you in the One.”

“Yes”, I agree. “I sensed a lack of love, and I turned outward to those around me.” I lean forward in excitement as I realize the depth of this discovery. “I experienced life as a human having the past knowledge of pure love, but I didn’t have pure love and so I sought validation outside myself to try to get that feeling to return. “

Bill smiled, a smile that was mirrored on the faces of everyone else in the group. “You got it, Sis!”

A being called Abby spoke from across the circle. “I began needing to understand loyalty from the heart rather than just from my head.”

Her words sent me drifting back to the life I just had experienced. I saw how loyalty was a positive experience for me at first, up until that loyalty led to resentment. My sense of loyalty always came with strings attached. What reward would I get for my loyalty? The answer should have been to express loyalty to the Highest aspect of my inner being, but I missed that goal somehow or other.

Abby must have had the same realization. “I could have stayed true to my soul connection with God,” she says, “so that my loyalty would mesh with my highest expectations. From this perspective I could be loyal without expecting any particular outcome.”

“Right,” I say. “If I co-create my life, than I co-create the pent up resentment of not always being able to express myself, of having a husband I perceived held me back, children that grew up without appreciation for all I had done for them, of having parents that would try to control my actions even after I became a mother.”

“I co-created the ending of my life as Abby,” she says.

“Yes! We create it all.” Suddenly my perception shifts to that of creator and no longer as a victim of circumstances. As Jessica, I created the perception of goodness and badness, not grasping that this dichotomy of opposites engenders destruction as well as creation.

A figure comes into our circle, glowing with translucent light as he expresses compassion in unspoken vibration. I look around me. All the others in the group are transfixed by him. His voice rings through my being as he speaks.

“It is the experiences of your soul and the experiences of all souls that gather into the great Over Soul. The experiences of conscious realities bring depth and understanding to the Source. In wisdom, knowledge leads the soul to a springboard from boundaries to ever-greater expansion beyond. The soul grows with all its experiences, peeling off the elements that are not assisting growth in Spirit. It is an unveiling. Gaining wisdom brings truth to experiences. In the worlds of time it is living in the Now. That is all there is. There are memories of the past, visions of the future, all wrapped up in the present moment. The power you are given is the power from your perception. This is your power as to how you perceive the experiences in the past, how you perceive your experiences in the future, and how you perceive yourself in your present situation."

We all meditate on his words as light ebbs and flows through us. The dancing vibrations of light and harmonizing sounds grow, rising to the celestial music. I grow into this flow of Spirit and hear Holy Sounds. I am no longer me. I am part of a great expansion of all that was, is, and will be. My conscious perception expands and I have compassion for those who do not yet perceive Love in its pure form. There are so many souls out there, caught in their creations. Weeping compassion flows from the depths within me. The pull of Spirit grows as I hear the music of God. The Flow of Source returns the self back to the Self through a great expansion of Love. I am no longer a single entity with boundaries or limits; I am of the One.

My group appears in this transcending flow and we again appear to one another. The faces and forms again appear as individual beings. I am again a separated me, from such all-encompassing love. I feel sad in this separation.

The figure in the middle places his hand on my head and peace that does pass all understanding comes over me. I sit quietly in this peace, knowing all life is of this One in this Great Love.

He turns into the middle of our circle and somehow seems to be facing all of us at the same time.

He speaks through his thoughts, but I see his lips move. 'Perhaps,' I think, 'I still need to see the visual of speech.'

"I am Rebc," he says. "There are many other, and even greater existences within yourself than the one you have just experienced. You still have a pull to physical form and you will continue to co-create into that reality, but you will find that as your vibrational awareness, grows, it will give you a greater awareness of the Source. Your deeper understanding is growing. You will transcend to that which you have always been a part of. There are still great existences you have not experienced and you will do so if you desire. You will experience these in your conscious reality when you are in vibrational alignment. There is only the flow of love from God, the Source, pouring fourth and returning to Source. In this great Love is the creation of all existences in perceived space and time. The Flow from the Source is, was, and will be for all who conceive of It. We are beings of the One; we are elements of God. Each form creates according to their conceived perception of Source, so your own perception of Source will be reflected in your creation. Deep within your being as you co-create on the physical level, is the desire to be back in the Flow of Source. The energy of Love is always there, calling fourth and bringing back to Source. You co-create your reality and recreate your perception of Source as you conceive of your relationship to the Flow of God. Any being, yourself included, wants to express to others the experience of their created reality. They can perceive the Flow of life with the pure love of God, flowing and returning back to Source. The pullback becomes stronger as the being comes closer to transcending lower dimensional reality. There is less resistance to the flow as the being nears completion of its intended expression with the physical realms. With this opening of harmonizing Spirit, the being moves freely, becoming One with the Light and Love of God. As you have experienced coming to deeper reality, there has to be a vibrational fit to your understanding. The Flow of God is without any judgments as to your choice of actions, thoughts, and emotions. The Source does not judge, for It Is and there cannot be separation in the One. If one judges, there is a distinction between what is there and what is not there, what is up and what is down, what is correct or what is not correct, what is good and what is not good, but in the Flow of Source there is no separation by solidification of points. The transcendence of the self to the Self is a transcendence of the one to the One. It is an understanding of all sides of what has been created. The realities are graced with Love in the Source. There can be no other but what is – Reality."

I sit in contemplation, listening, as my being opens to the conceptions presented. My heart opens to the energy of love that is transferred through his being. His presence opens my understanding. I ask in my mind who is Rebc, and he smiles upon me. The others seem already to know.

He smiles yet again. "I am from other realms of God. I am from other existences of much finer vibration. There are even finer vibrations closer to the God Source. I perceive there is no ending to the transformation to greater spiritual growth to God."

There is a deep silence as we sit quietly. Rebc rests in the middle of the circle. "We will now face an element within ourselves that is a part of the plan of God which many times we do not want to see. It collaborates in our inner belief systems many times as a separate being of power. It is not. It exists in a form that develops as we have contrasting experiences of realities. A side that is necessary to bring the contrast of light to fruitions."

I find myself closing my eyes, as a new scenario unfolds before me. This is a scene where I feel deep emotion. The part of me that is feeling the emotion is separate from the side of me that already knows its outcome. This other side of me is crying to be heard. I see my deep selfishness, as I blame my partner for not giving me what I feel I need. Then I see myself not caring if people get hurt as I justify what I need now. I see myself denouncing my mother for having caused the woes in my life, and I see that I blame her because I do not want to face my own responsibility. I see myself squander my body to satisfy my need to feel good. I see myself fighting my way to the top regardless of the pain of others, and I justify my actions along the way. I hear a voice in my head crying to be heard, speaking to my better sense as I wallow in self-pity. Deep inside, I know my true motives, but I cover that ugly side with excuses. I hear a voice pleading with me to look closer at what I am doing, and I see the one underlying cause of pain in all my life situations. My soul weeps at that pain, because it vibrates into the souls of others. Selfish vibrational actions attracts selfish actions in other beings. No matter whether it is greed, lust, or revenge—all find vibrational sameness. Just as magnetism is a law in the physical realm, so too is the action of this energy. I see each element grow in strength to manifest greater realities as they project outward. It begins to seem as if an outside force is creating inharmonic realities, stopping the Flow of Source. Each time that connection with God is blocked, my actions—and the actions of all others—become more desperate, many times reaching into the dark side for answers.

I open my eyes and see Rebc looking into my heart.

"Part of you has kept you from greater light in life. You turned away to try to escape the pain in your soul. The great purification is simply taking away those things that no longer serve your soul, and then you are able to be in a vibrational connection to God. There is only the Flow of Love from the Highest to the Highest. It is the transcriber of all life forms. Purify your thoughts and emotions to see the purity of life. No life form, including yourself, can remove itself from the realm of God, but you can choose not to pay attention. I am here to urge you to create, to put your attention on what vibrates with your soul. Your reality vibrates with the forms of life in your conscious spotlight. There are other avenues you can follow, but those do not have to be part of your choice. You can remove yourself from enjoyment, or you can choose to be truly, deeply involved in the activities of a life you have entered into, for you now know there are other choices your could have. You can know in your conscious reality at all times that you are of the Higher Being, you are in the Flow of God. You can do this as you spotlight your reality."

Shanderia returned and sat behind me on the swirls of a light chair. I noticed other beings sitting behind those in the circle too.

"I must leave you now," Rebc said, and I felt his loving goodbye resonate within my heart center. Love poured from each of us in the circle, flowing out to him.

"In the Light and Love of the Great Spirit I depart and Blessings from the Highest!" A brilliant light bursts forth from his being, shining as he departs.

A being behind Luke speaks to our minds. "Do you wish to transform to another form for experience in the physical realm?"

With this question a picture comes into my mind, of a life of servitude to others, breaking beyond the bounds of the close circle I had experienced in previous lifetimes.

I look around at the others and see that they too are in deep thought, and I assume they each are seeing their own pictures of what could be. I cannot think of anything more enjoyable now than serving others through my heart connecting with the Flow of God. I know now the passion of my heart will be my guide as I transform to another life experience.

Shanderia speaks to me, "Your choice will bring you to greater understanding of love. Through service you will be given greater sight to the underlying truth of life. When you come from your deepest self you can truly serve others as you serve yourself, and you honor others as you honor yourself."

"Yes. Shanderia. I feel in myself the great reward I seek will be in service to others. This will be the path I follow, the Will of God."

Shanderia motions for me to follow her. We enter what seems to be a viewing room.

"In what type of service would you like to manifest in your next form?"

"I have great compassion in my heart for those wishing for something greater, outside of their existent lives. My understanding for those who wish to grow into the Light comes from my heart. I will have compassion for other's plight in their search for greater knowledge, as I have understanding of their created blindness.

"You will see the Light of God in many situations that will challenge you. But that challenge is necessary both for your own growth and for others."

"Others? What do you mean?"

"They will learn from seeing how you meet those challenges."

"What about this group of souls here with me now, Shanderia? Will they be in my experience as I enter the next life form?"

"Some will work out their experiences in other ways, but those who want to be of service will join you so that they can assist you or you can assist them. Some of this assistance will be obvious, and will be perceived as a blessing, but you may perceive others as a hindrance. Know, though, that all will assist you on your path, in the same way that you will assist them on theirs. You see, you are greater than a linear, singular being. There is a vast expanse of your Self you cannot truly see when living in lower dimensional lives, just as there are other experiences being created in other realms by your High Self."

What she says is far beyond my comprehension at this time, so I simply let the thoughts drift through me. I'm sure I will understand them sometime in the future.

"What about angels, Shanderia?" I sense they are around me yet I have not experienced them in my transition. Of course, as soon as I think this, I see angelic beings flying around us, in tune with the music of God's Light. "Oh!" I say. "They don't have wings!"

Shanderia seems amused by this. "They don't need wings, my dear. What you see is the light of pure love energy pulsing around them."

"Why, then, does everyone say angels have wings?"

"Most people need a physical reference in order to understand. The energy flow from behind them appeared to them as wings, since they also defy physical gravity."

That makes sense to me. The angels are translucent and so very bright from afar. They smile and chant, surrounded by the music of the spheres and the flow of God.

"As you see, my curious one, they are here in your reality if you ever wish to see them. Their experience is a different path than your path. Their dimension of reality is but a thought form away. Their path has taken them into other expressions of God's Love."

"Why can't I see them all the time?"

"There is much talk in many of your earthly religions about angels, stories of light beings helping with human dilemmas or of humans awakening in Spirit, but there are many times we do not get into unconscious alignment with our conscious desires. In other words, dear one, it is only our limited sight that restricts us from seeing angels. The beauty of the angelic world is there for us to experience if we truly wish to experience it."

"You mean I chose not to see them when I was expressing myself as Jessica Ann?"

"Yes. You limited yourself and kept within the limits you chose. As one grows in awareness from the realm of the physical to the spiritual reality, one can begin to see beyond those self-created boundaries. We become aware of other dimensions, of other beings, of the transient nature of the being we have imagined. This can open our sight, not only to angels but to countless other possibilities in God's creation."

I took in what Shanderia was saying to me as I watched the angels, living in their translucent splendor. I found it hard to remember what I had been like as Jessica Ann. It took so much effort to recall physical experiences. I think and begin to question everything I experienced, asking for reasons, giving excuses, coming up with flawed explanations.

Suddenly the angels are gone from sight. "What happened?"

"You are the creator of your reality. You began to think of limits and what that would mean to your reality. It would mean limits that would not be found in the angelic realms. These limits cause issues of pain since there 'seems' to be less love and less energy of life. The cause and effect of pain starts a new path with its desire to alleviate that pain."

Shanderia seems to project a new sight to me. I see earth with an underlying flow of energy—Light and Sound that harmonize into a continual creation of reality. I realize that the flow of Spirit into all creation is always there. Each element takes in the Flow of Spirit and creates the form that is passed through its visualized filter. Each element of earth is alive with the Spirit; animals, rocks, plants, air; all of them sparkle with their conscious manifestation. Some life is more aware of this creation process than other life forms. Yet each form transitions the energy of God to its vibrational harmony.

"Do humans have a greater freedom to manifest the flow of Spirit?"

"You have this freedom," she tells me, "but with it comes a responsibility to keep the vehicle open. Animals, like people, have contracts and instincts. There is always choice, but the choices are not always conscious. Sometimes the energy flow is so entrenched that it takes great effort of energy to change a particular path. As in physics, an object in motion will continue in that motion unless energy is exerted to stop or change the motion. So it is with manifested energy."

I can see the concept of karma being reflected through this insight. Karma is put into motion by manifestation. It is only with great effort, energy, one can change that karmic action in another direction or stop that karmic action altogether.

Shanderia takes my hand, and I am shaken out of the deep insight.

She says, "It is now time for you to make a decision."

We come, instantly, to a beautiful room where cream-colored light forms the walls. In the middle of the room, there is a circle made up of columns. Between these columns appears a wall of mist.

"Your soul will now decide the manifested direction you wish to go. This room will allow you to see many possibilities, and you may review your karmic conscious patterns before you decide how to manifest. You will pick one or more themes for your projected life experiences. The theme your energy resonates with is 'service'. The type of service you look for is a consciously based spiritual life. You may choose other themes such as greater self-confidence or facing challenges with greater courage of soul. The viewing room is to allow you to decide within your own soul self." She smiled as if to herself. "As you go through your physical life, this knowledge will usually be hidden from your conscious sight."

I ponder her words as the mists between the two columns begin moving into shapes. Figures begin to appear before us and I see myself, but not myself. It is another life that could be, a life where I appear as a female but I am different than Jessica Ann. I am still in human form and it appears to be on the planet earth. That woman before me appears more confident in her posture and facial expression. She is in a life that is much simpler in technology than the last life I chose. She is teaching or at least talking to a group of people. I feel astonished as they listen intently. If I choose this life, I will no longer be an introvert! She wears simple clothing—a basic tunic shirt and loose fitting pants with a cord holding them up. Her boots are tied with a cord around the ankles. All the men and women have shoulder-length hair cut in a blunt style. The land around them is lightly wooded, with rolling hills and patches of bushes. I observe no buildings.

As I analyze the visual before me in the mists, Shanderia says, "My child, this is only one of the possibilities you may choose. As we have discussed, your goal in this upcoming life will be of service. Here," and she gestured to the scene before me, "you are a teacher assisting others to learn about themselves. The life you are looking at is one you intentionally brought up yourself. It is still upon the planet earth, during a contemplative time when the earth energy is cleansing itself and balancing into harmonic resonance supporting all life forms. There is high technology, but it is compartmentalized so there will be more balance with life. Technology in this lifetime is used for transportation to and from earth, around the earth, in some medical procedures, in growing sustenance for the people, and in some educational patterns. Otherwise technology is discouraged from use."

"But, but…" I stutter.

"I know you are asking when and how this could exist. Although we do not need time here," and she gestures gracefully around her, "but on an earth time-line it is conceived in the future from your last life. You will find energy calmer and deeply contemplative. Such internalization is necessary for the human species to survive upon the earth. It will be considered a spiritual awakening. There was great upheaval to get to this position. The result is that the leaders in this time guide people toward inner as well as outer prosperity. Human consciousness is striving to find itself in a balance of physical survival through spiritual sightedness. You have, in your energy intent, chosen to be a teacher. The training is somewhat like a branding, showing that you are a spiritual advisor/leader in the community. Through your training you will be able to sustain your heightened consciousness as you talk to those around you. It is a very interesting life you choose."

As Shanderia spoke, I melted into the life, feeling the woman's feelings as she spoke to the group. What a crystal-clear clarity she is experiencing as she teaches. I begin to see what she sees; I look out at the group of people, and I see bands of love streaming everywhere. I see light beams of love intertwine the people and myself. I look to the land and see it is as I had seen this woman from the spiritual realms, a sparkling reflection of light with energy-emitting auras of color. The words she speaks come from what she sees and the people listen.

I suddenly feel a hand on my shoulder. Shanderia is standing next to me.

"As your energy manifests this scene for a potential future experience, your consciousness quickly melts into its life energy form. You are very drawn to this life experience. Your desire to serve and your openness to the Flow of Light are culminating to manifest this possibility. As you have gone through lives of illusion, with indulgences of pain and fear, you can now see that you have reached beyond this state of being. You know you are connected with Light and Love of God. Nothing outside of you will change that reality."

"Is this life I've seen predestined before it happens?"

"It is not completely predestined. It will always be up to you and how you wish to respond to given situations. Each moment you will choose either to align with the manifestation or not. It is a structured manifestation you enter into. You will decide to accept the given moment and follow the path or create new paths. It is freedom we all have. You will find the higher reaches from your soul as reflecting God's finer vibrational path in every moment. It can uplift your spirit into much higher realms of being. You will find that your soul will remember this. It is why we listen inside ourselves. The answer is within us as our soul talks through many different forms."

"So nothing is decided ahead of time? It's all up to me?"

She paused to think for a moment. "During your life there will be what we call markers, where certain experiences will need to manifest around you. At those times you will decide from whence to go. These markers may come as opportunities or just as often as challenges. You decide where to go from these created markers. If you create deep love, it will be reflected back to you. Given moments can pass if you do not desire them, some will stay and grow as you open up to them. The potential of life's creation is endless. The only limits will be the limits you put upon yourself. This is co-creating; you will open up to God's Spirit as it manifests through you. It will be your choice to open–or not to open—to this Flow. If you choose the first path, it will lead you to much greater levels of understanding and love. If you choose the second path, it will lead you to cycles of pain and desperation."

"How clear will those choices be? Will I know what's happening to me?"

"Your experiences in your consciousness will seem very real to you. Within you are all the experiences of your various lives—ones that you have lived, and as time is circular, will live, and are living too. Your individual experiences also have aspects of the group culminations of experiences."

As she says this, a circle of people appears around me.

"These souls are your inner circle. You've agreed to create experiences common with your group. This is a predestined agreement, one that you all made before experiencing any of your physical lives."

We all close our eyes and hold our hands up in a meditative pose. We stand still as the mists merge into a new scenario. It begins to show lives where some of these people are in the crowd I was talking to earlier. One is my mother, another is my brother, and there is Jack as my partner. Oh, this is a beautiful life, calm and easy to contact spirit in my everyday existence. Yet this life holds challenges to learn. I see myself getting tremendous headaches. The headaches are so bad I must retire to bed. I notice the headaches getting worse. I see that it is through my inner contemplation that I subdue these headaches and get free of the pain. In this life, I finally get control of myself in confidence. I can discipline myself to action beyond limits that stopped me in previous lives. I notice how the confidence comes with knowingness inside me. I am born with a knowing that there is no dependence upon outside influences to thank or blame. It just is. In this moment, I feel strong in the Flow of God within. It grows in seeing the Flow within others and life all around. The confidence is the place within myself I see the greater reality so I am not as easily swayed by other realities that are not conducive to what I want or need to accomplish. I go into the silence to listen and learn; I go into the silence to be.

"This life looks too perfect," I say. "Too easy."

"Do not fear," Shanderia says with an undercurrent of amusement. "There will be many challenges to upset that inner confidence, to swing the spotlight away so you will see yourself as a victim and not as a spiritual warrior."

"I think I can stand up to such challenges."

"Do you? The vibrations will become more and more refined. You will need to take the higher road in order to resist them and you must strengthen your vibrations in the Flow in all situations. Only then will it become easier. Only then will your karmic energy travel the path to God."

I look around to see the group that is now standing with me. I observe the scene between the pillars and I turn back to the swirling mists. I see my guides around me and feel their supported vibrations. I see that all the ones in the group have their own experiences with their own guides around them. The guides will assist, but only if asked by the person.

"That is right," Shanderia says, and I know she has perceived my thoughts. "These are not angels. You can choose to interact with your guides as little or as much as you want to.

"Does everyone see something different?" I ask her.

She lowers her voice. "Some see things differently and some similarly. Each is creating their own manifestation. There is common vision, individual vision, and sometimes group vision compliant with all involved. There are many ways to manifest. Now you are creating individually with a group manifestation."

"I'm not sure I understand you."

"Think of it as a line of attraction by vibrations. This attraction is your consciousness reflecting out a vision it sees from within itself. The others will have their perception from their own vibrational consciousness. You see it is an individual creation in conjunction with a group creation."

"But how can I influence my will over someone else so they agree with my sense of what I want to create?"

"In the beauty of creating with conscious energy you cannot ever exert your will over someone else. Perhaps there are scenes where it seems one person forces his will onto another. In the greater depths of vibration, though, it is agreed to happen. The agreement is within and the reflection is the result of that agreement from both sides. Therefore, when you try to make someone do your will, they will use your will in agreement to do their will. There can be a being with a vibrational match to your desire who will enter your reality to interact with you and you with them."

"You're just saying everything is predestined."

"No, my dear. If you want to change a path you will need to change your vibrations in your thoughts and emotions first to attract what you do want to have in your experiences. Great paranoia will enter into leaders with perceived power over others. On a deeper level they know that the power over others is never truly theirs to have. It is vibrational agreement. In their deeper, usually unconscious, understanding of reality they feel like they are losing personal control, their power. As their focus is outside themselves at this time, they become desperate to maintain their power, their illusion of control over others. This is true of many life scenarios, and it happens whenever the reality of the outside creation is greater than the source from whence it came."

I look at the group before me, in their beautiful robes of light. I feel the Divine within them as I feel it within myself. It is my reality and my choice to spotlight the Flow of God in what I perceive.

"There is nothing that is outside this flow of light and love," as I contemplate, "and it all creates through manifestation and returns to the Purity of Divine Love."

"Greetings, Madeka," Shanderia says as a male entity appears beside her, and I feel a swirling flow of the Eternal Source.

"The contrast," he says, "between what you now feel and the challenges you will face in your upcoming life, is the setting for many experiences. This will bring about growth as you peel away the layers that no longer serve you. All that we experience is according to our desires. As you enter into the coarser vibrational realities, your life purpose will be shaded from your spotlight. This is our chance to learn how to be with Divine reality again. It is letting go of your preconceived notions and unwanted teachings to find the Oneness in all limitless reality. You will experience your individuality in concordance with the Divine Flow. Not until you feel in balance with universal energies will you know peace within your soul."

As Mandeka speaks these words, I am surrounded with love.

"We are always in the Light and Love experiencing the Higher Power from God Source. It leads to clearer sight for our path in life and beyond. The agreements we make before our physical births will nudge us at certain times in our lives. They will awaken our thoughts to take action. The expanding soul deep within remembers the agreements. This gives the personality a guided road map, so we know when to turn or to stop and change course. It is our agreements that will be reminders for the soul to see new possibilities open to its present way of life. You will feel strong desires to find a way to fulfill such a nudge. If you follow that road map, your soul will find its right way."

I see the agreements I am making with Luke. We will meet soon after we are born. We will recognize the connection we have, and that connection will feel familiar and warm. The relationship with Luke will be peaceful and loving, without the many obstacles that occurred in our last life together. But I can see that I will have a great deal of challenge dealing with society as a whole. Their rules will be contrary to my deeper knowing. I will need to rise above those rules to follow from within my soul. I will deal with many different people, but the greatest challenge, and the greatest teacher of this experience will be John, who was my husband in my previous life on earth. He will want to maintain the stagnant behavior of society. He will not see the energy that flows through life, trying to changes its vibrational patterns to a finer pattern. He will want to grab hold and solidify the pattern as it is, and this will be his lesson. I will be focusing intently upon having society rise above this solidification into greater possibilities. I will have an ally, though, someone besides Luke. Mandeka will want to assist me with all his heart, turning against his family to do so. His family will be in the ruling class and as such will want society to remain in stagnant power rule.

I see the light energy swirl around us making our manifestation of experience into a reality. We are taken from a boundless experience to more and more boundaries. We are taken from the expansive realm of just knowing to a conscious feeling of foggy thoughts. We are taken from an all-encompassing love to a narrowly defined love. I feel myself slowing down so much I turn to look back from where I came. I sink down, down, down. I know it is the vibrational energy slowing to meet the physical reality. I know this is the experience of entering a human form; I have done this many times. It is a baby's body in a womb. I let my energy merge in its slower vibration to cellular matching. I am aligning with a girl child. Shanderia helps me through this process, and I know she has been beside me throughout many lifetimes.

I look out from myself in spirit form and see that some others are not so comfortable entering into their human forms. They are hovering above the bodies of the baby and mother. They will enter when they are ready to adjust their vibration to its form. I see a soul that has changed its intentions. It will go back to the Higher Realms of God, although the humans here in this lifetime will see that exit as a death. Then, another soul agrees to enter its human form. There are many souls desiring to have this experience, but it must be with agreed alignment to find the correct life form for its proper intentional experience. There are no errors to be made, only the reality of the present manifesting experiences. I now experience the energy complete itself into my new baby form. There is still energy that is of the 'I', not participating in the physical experience. It will remain in the Higher Realms of Light, and be available to guide the physical form, sometimes appearing as a sunset, the distant call of a bird, a gentle shower on parched ground. Each of these will allow the physical form to see glimpses of itself in the Realm closer to God Source.

Suddenly the limits begin to transform the calm placidity of Self to the self, and I ache with many desires. The baby form makes its basic desires known and receives its fulfillment in the womb. DNA intertwines with the energy of the Flow, creating earth form. The speed is confusing at first, as energy slows to synchronize with its manifestation. I have a feeling of lack and a need for my desires to be fulfilled.

I am in central Russia. The expanse of consciousness narrows until I am a baby being nourished within a dark warm womb. Unlike many other lives I have lived, I do not feel a strong energy bonding with the woman whose body nourishes mine. I do not have the strands of energy connection to her being. I choose to be connected to another on the earth plane. I feel my energy expanding out to this other person I will later call mother. I feel my energy intertwining into her energy field. I hover a moment and know that her vibrations coordinate to my vibrations. I will be in her life soon. The agreement to these interactions was made on a soul level. The womb I am in will give birth to me, and I will be taking her DNA, but another, who will teach me her wisdom and ways of life, will raise me.

The woman giving birth, Luba, has agreed to do this. In her agreement lingers the nagging thought of not keeping this child. She has kept all her other children, and none have been taken away. This child is different in that she is experiencing such sadness with her pregnancy, she is tired, and she does not want to keep the child, but still... "Wait three days before you decide," say the doctors.

She is in agreement with her soul as she lies in the bed after giving birth. She is old and feels exhausted. She does not want to have yet another child with insurmountable problems–deformities, lack of success, failure to thrive. There are few ways to succeed in this society. She thinks her only choice is to leave now and not look back. Her head knows it is right, but her heart longs to keep this child. In all aspects of life there is free will and there are other choices. I know that my energy is a strong force in Luba's thought process. I know she feels tired and depressed. I feel her love for her children, but her body is exhausted from the struggle of trying to survive in her world.

She is forty-seven when she gives birth. She makes up her mind to walk away from this responsibility. She will return to her life cleaning the school ten hours a day; at least she had a job. Her husband and children have jobs off and on. Some forget to get their work papers renewed. Luba's mother and mother-in-law have said they will not help raise another child, chanting the thought to give her up this child. Boris, her husband shows very little interest. I feel the distress vibrating from her being. My energy form still can hover above the physical form, as I still have some freedom to come and go between dimensions before I solidify my spotlight into the physical reality. The labor is short but the child comes out and Luba knows that there are problems. For a short time, the baby does not respond. Suddenly the baby breathes and cries, but the doctor fears there has been brain damage. Luba cannot deal with another such child. The pain of it digs deep into her soul and she signs the papers to allow her child to be adopted out. She must take care of herself and her other children. The finer vibrational self that I am still hovers above the child, beyond space and time. The conscious easy access will soon end. The spotlight to the Oneness will soon end. It will be a remembered dream. It will lie hidden in the aspects of the being. The child will later see the infinite Oneness through meditation, contemplation, or other forms of thought that will lead it to transcendence. This identity is no longer Jessica Ann, and there is no longer any free access to transcendence. Such memories will be erased from conscious thought. It is no longer in dimensions of being in the all-encompassing time but in a reality of the future and past. I integrate fully into the body of the baby. I am now in time and space.

The baby awakes as it struggles through the birth canal into a harsh reality. She gasps for her first breath but panics when she finds that the breath is painful. She is cold. She is hungry. She is tired. What happened to the warmth where she used to be? Her limbs are heavy. There is no longer any uplifting feeling of love all around her. She is alone. The light that used to be so soft and gentle is now glaring and hurtful. Why has this happened to her?

There must be Love somewhere, but her baby mind cannot find the words for it. Still, something seems to envelop her and she finds a moment's peace, knowing that Love that passes all understanding will guide her in this limited realm.

She feels pain. The soul energy pulls back and hovers over the baby's body, for there is a doubt whether to leave the physical form and go back, but then it continues to solidify itself to make this journey through life. The child sees blurry lights and shadows. She feels a scratchiness against her skin as the nurse wraps her in a blanket. All the messages coming from her five physical senses merge into her consciousness. As the experiences intensify, she knows that she has begun her new physical life. The awareness of experiences will be through this body.

This body which cannot seem to breathe correctly. They clamp something over her mouth and nose, and she begins to breathe with its assistance. After a time, she can take normal breaths. "There appears to be no major damage," the doctor says, but there seems to be some doubt in his eyes. They cut the cord, wash her eyes, bathe and wrap her. The mother falls asleep as the baby is brought to the newborn section of the hospital. She is fed, cleaned and placed with many other babies in a lighted room. The mother disappears the next day. The Child Welfare office is called. They try to contact a relative without success. The baby is taken to an orphanage.

There is a reason for all of this, but the baby does not know. Her soul has forgotten the agreement she made before her birth.

In the orphanage there are so many children. She feels the need to touch others with her energy. She cries for the great feeling of Love, reaching out with the energy of her body. It is only in her sleep that her soul languishes in the realm of pure Light and Love. She finds comfort as a feeling of love appears in her world. It is not seen with her blurry eyes but clearly within her mind. An angel's light shines to her and other children around her. They are all in awe of this presence. The orphanage workers think the children have settled down and are sleeping.

One day she is taken in the arms of a form and put into a big box where the air smells different, and the sounds are strange and new. There is a discomfort of coldness on her face. As she travels in the car she feels a touch and falls asleep with this comforting feeling. She moves her eyes back and forth, which helps lull her to sleep. She holds a corner of her blanket and fades away.

She awakes crying, hungry. There are many others crying too. She cannot see them but hears their cries. After a while an orphanage worker touches her again. This one will be her special one because she is the one that makes sounds to her and sings to her as she holds her. She is given nourishment from a bottle. She returns to her sleep area and finds the corner of her blanket. Her body longs to put more in her mouth, but she learns not to cry when she sometimes does not get enough to eat. She wants to touch one of the other babies, but this darn body won't cooperate.

The first time she is put on a potty seat, she finds that stuff comes out of her body. When she is picked up she looks down and sees what she left behind. She is very excited to see what she made.

She discovers her legs and feet. She touches another child and the other child touches her.

The big one that talks to her makes her feel happy. She smiles and flaps her legs and arms. In response, the big one makes sounds to her, touches her, smiles at her. She feels the energy exchanging. These caretakers are older women who need the work. They have raised children and know what is needed to keep them as healthy as the scant resources allow. Their pragmatism is stronger than emotions. They work so more children will survive, but the system is not on their side.

As the baby sleeps, her soul expands to a greater understanding. She sees many other souls choosing this beginning. Many of their destinies will be worlds apart in their experiences. She can see many lighted figures around the souls here. She does not give a name to her special presence, but knows it is female, mother. The form is fluid and she feels the love from the streaming light traveling through and around her. As she sleeps, she listens to the sacred sounds bathed in harmony.

She is awakened by another baby screaming in the dark, a scream so intense that she is frightened at first. But then she feels love energy flowing from her. She cries, for she knows no other way to express her distress.

A big one comes and takes the dying baby out of the room.

The baby finds comfort in her routine of waking activities and sleeping dreams. Her big one often gives her an extra hug and a smile. One day she is taken into a room filled with bright colors, where a new woman picks her up, a woman the baby has never seen before.

This caretaker is different; light comes from inside her and illuminates the baby. Thoughts come flooding in and she smiles. The baby appears to be in awe of this woman as she looks at her with a smile. The baby sees the light beings smiling with her. She knows this is the one. The big one puts out her hand. She grabs on to her finger and stands up. It seems so natural. She takes her first steps. She is nine months old. Oh this new sensation is so incredible. She enjoys how this makes her feel. Deep in her soul she knows Shanderia is whispering that a new step in this life's journey is about to begin.

The other caretaker comes to get her, taking her back to familiarity. The new sensations will be in her thoughts tonight. She feels her new caretaker give her a hug and the light swirls from her chest. Oh, this feeling is strong, deep love always is. In her sleep bed she curls her corner of her blanket and hugs it good night.

As she sleeps the night, her soul energy wants to ground further in the connection with physical form. The stream of energy from her soul star swirls to the earthstar in brilliant rays. Her light body is alive in this renewal of energy.

In her dream of her light body she calls out to the caretaker, the woman that will change her course. "Hurry! Come and get me."

Over the years, Brooklyn's love for her mommy deepens. She explores the world and finds people that love her back. She feels secure. Yet lurking in the background is a fear of being left behind and it is out of her control.

Although Brooklyn does not realize it, Shanderia stands beside her and whispers that all is well. Brook hears the echo of Shanderia's voice and begins to cry, and her mother holds her tightly, rocking her to a deep sleep. She does not know why little Brooklyn is crying. She only knows that she loves this child whole-heartedly.

Years later, Brooklyn is walking home one evening from band rehearsal. The frosty fall night is clear and crisp. She looks up to the stars, full of wonder, beauty, and mystery. They shine, Brooklyn knows, upon many known and unknown realities. The life out beyond this earth planet twinkles at her, and she feels a flowing light that is reflecting from her heart. There is one star that seems to come right into her. She looks up at the light and remembers her oneness with the Light and Love of All.

In Oneness, any sense of separation, lack, or pain is washed away, for God is all; there can be no condemnation or separation.

Brooklyn kneels down in this sacred moment and weeps tears of understanding. She feels herself reaching beyond Brooklyn, reaching beyond the boundaries of this lifetime. She knows from deep within her heart and soul, that deeper realities exist, intertwining us all in great Oneness of energy. Her body is alive with energy. She touches pure Love, pure Light.

Silence.

She walks away knowing she will share this understanding with others who wish to see, who wish to understand, the reality beyond their physical eyes. It is a sight we all see, when we are ready. It is the Light Beyond the Stars!

Valerie Savage lives in Wisconsin with her daughter, two dogs, and three fish. Enjoyably, she is in the beginning stages of retirement. Valerie is starting a spiritual direction program and further in-depth practices as she continues to expand her undertanding of the Truth behind the veil.

Notes from the Author:

In me lie the answers that I seek in the whispered emptiness of night. Here lies the burning energy that is the 'I', the soul. Here lies the flowing renewal of God's greater realms. Here lies the great flow of love that creates life anew. The seeming emptiness is a block that is not real to my Greater Self. Emptiness fades away with my growing awareness of myself in relation to God.

The energy body connected with the energy aura of the ethereal realms is where I can start to place my awareness. To view life through my energy body is to view life with the flow of angelic music. I see the energy body more clearly as I practice this connection. The energy body grows in greater reflection of the ethereal realms. When I open to this newer, greater reality, it becomes my brightest spotlight.

How can I not see the truer nature of my being as I practice searching the greater depths of who I am? The truth lies within all life. I am nature, and nature is me. As I study the true substance of nature I delve into the truth behind the veil. Here emerges a hidden reality beneath the physical reality.

John 14:2 "In my Father's house are many rooms."

My physical body is a reflection from the unseen world, hidden only by my awareness. The unseen dimensional reality that is there, visible if I wish to know it.

Let me reflect upon the awareness I can see from my ethereal body. Take the thoughts that have been filtered in, take the causes that are manifesting, give movement with my emotions, and I am creating the physical reality, I am stepping out onto this earth.

This is why I keep doing the rituals, the personal searches, the reflective understandings. I keep cleansing the filter as the purity of God's flow comes through me. I keep purifying the filter so the reflection of God will be purer and purer to the world. It is in simplicity I see the complexity clearly.

I can have pain from perceived past rejections, anger from perceived injustices, guilty from perceived wrong doings, or perceived self-righteous actions. I can have clogged filters from accumulated thoughts from families, societies, civilizations, and humanness, and I can let any misgiving hinder my flow and clog my filter. Or I do not have to let any of this happen.

As I choose to cleanse the filter in my pursuit of greater understanding of God, I come to see the grandness of my true nature in God's flow of Holy love. I come to see that nothing can hinder this process unless I allow it to be so.

The scientist discovers the quark, the small elemental particle that makes up matter. The mystics say there is a field of Light from Spirit that is connecting us into Holey Oneness. It is agreed that there are invisible realities making up the sensed reality. There is change through the movement of evolution; in spirit, it is movement toward the God Source. There is no conflict, only greater understanding from different paths leading to the One.

Life becomes lifted further and further toward the Source. It is from this movement that leads to an understanding of what is. It begins to answer the questions of so many whys, how comes, and what to do now. I concentrate upon my Divine Self as I grow in my understanding of living. Namaste; the God in me sees the God in you. The Christ in me sees the Christ in you. This is the holiness in which life sees itself in all of Life. I concentrate upon the Divine Self and I begin to see the Christ in all situations. I begin to pray in my thoughts for the highest and best good in all. I begin to understand that there is an ethereal reality vibrating through my physical reality. I concentrate upon God in my Divine Self as I grow ever deeper.

I must make this journey into myself. Others cannot make it for me. Others cannot tell it to me. I must make my own way to this greater understanding, to my highest and best good within myself. There can be guides to show a better path, but in the end, it is my own journey to find the Divinity within my Divine Self. I know I will find the blessings of God that reign within my heart. With grace, I know I shall have peace that passes all understanding. It is within Divine Being that I will find love beyond all words of expression.

That is why making someone take a certain path from the outside will not last in the end unless the other is willing to take it within their own thought and emotional paradigm and to make it part of their energy being. That is why force conversions will only work some of the time and usually on those who are weak within their own belief system. These people will sway with outside influences depending upon persuasive measures; they will not come from their inner knowing. Then there are souls who only see their inside belief system that is built and solidified into resistance from any outside influence for growth. They, too, lose contact with their inner voice.

It is important for me as I make this journey to have an open heart/mind to life around and within. It is in my wisdom as I learn with fluidity, making my way through living and growing at the highest and best good, bound with a strong connection to God's flow of love, goodness, grace, light, and life. I know there will be empty nights, regretful nights, nights of despair, but those nights will happen less often as I open to the radiance of God's loving flow.

Let a compassionate sight keep me from being caught up in the frustration of everyday life that could take over my thoughts, emotions and body.

> I pray now with love and an open heart. I pray to have the insight to see all people in their highest Self, all Divine love of God, as I am Divine love of God. I pray to bring this understanding to all my relationships. I pray to bring this understanding to my creation of life as I live it. I pray to practice in my silence and in my loudness of living. I pray now to cleanse my filter for greater sight, allowing the Flow of God to come through me. I pray that I may be a messenger of God's flowing, swirling energy of vibrational wisdom. This I pray to stay in the Divine Self, to express the Divine Love, in Life Eternal.
>
> This I Pray.

Valerie

CPSIA information can be obtained
at www.ICGtesting.com
Printed in the USA
LVHW012348081021
699972LV00004B/109

9 780989 714259